craft
COCKTAILS

A Collection of Recipes & Stories
from Ireland's Leading
Spirit Makers

Monika Coghlan

ABOUT THE AUTHOR

Monika Coghlan is a Food and Drink Photographer by day, and a Wine and Cocktail Enthusiast by night.

She has completed several mixology courses where she learnt principles behind cocktail making, and is currently mastering Level 3 at the globally recognised Wine and Spirit Education Trust (WSET).

Monika strongly supports local Irish spirit makers and has visited many distilleries in Ireland while working on imagery and cocktail recipes for their brands.

Check out Monika's work on www.pepperazzi.ie and Instagram @pepperazzi_ie

Copyright © Monika Coghlan 2020

Published by Monika Coghlan

Hardback ISBN 978-1-8382060-0-0
eBook ISBN 978-1-8382060-1-7

Recipes created by featured spirit makers and Monika Coghlan unless otherwise stated.

Stories created by featured spirit makers.

Photography by Monika Coghlan

Photos on p. 15, 33, 48, 85, 131 and 146 taken at Bar 1661 in Dublin
Photos on p. 20, 36, 53, 71, 114, 134 and 151 taken at Cask in Cork
Photos on p. 28 and 136 by Caolan Barron, courtesy of Waterford Distillery
Photo on p. 80 courtesy of Clonakilty Distillery

Design and illustrations by Aoibhne Hogan
Edited and proofread by Brenda Murphy
Indexed by Kate Murphy
Printed and bound in Poland by BZ Graf

A CIP catalogue record for this book is available from the British Library.

TABLE OF CONTENTS

INTRODUCTION

Cocktail culture in Ireland is constantly evolving and cocktail consumption, as well as the appreciation of quality drinks, is fast growing. The number of premium and award-winning distilleries, big and small, is on the rise and so is people's awareness and recognition of Irish-made craft spirits. Let's continue to support them as choosing local is more important now than ever before.

With this book, you can become a home mixologist and create bespoke drinks using local Irish spirits and accessible ingredients from the comfort of your own home.

This stylish collection of over 50 craft cocktail recipes and fascinating stories from Ireland's leading spirit makers will inspire you to try something new and make beautifully unique drinks for every occasion.

From classic favourites with a modern twist to quirky creations, they will be a showstopper at your dinner party, Christmas celebration or quiet night in. Get your friends and family together to celebrate by creating delicious concoctions while supporting fantastic Irish brands.

A craft cocktail is so much more than a simple alcoholic drink. It's a combination of complementing and contrasting flavours that are perfectly balanced with a well planned choice of seasonal ingredients. It's an experience to be shared. It's about togetherness, entertaining and celebrating life. Let me share my passion for cocktail making with you. Let the cocktail culture bring us together. The Irish way.

Enjoy responsibly. Sláinte!

'To nurture and grow our much loved Irish drinks industry requires a continuous challenge to educate, celebrate and inspire. We need to learn the histories of our whiskeys, gins and poitíns, give them more limelight and share how our bartenders shake each of them up. Thankfully, a book now exists that can do all that.

Monika Coghlan's *Craft Cocktails* is a timely study into some of the finest spirits to be currently found on the island of Ireland, captured with sumptuous photography and recipes from some of our best distilleries and bars.'

Oisín Davis, Great Irish Beverages

Raise
a
Glass
to
the
Spirit
of
Collaboration

TULLAMORE D.E.W. WHISKEY

Tullamore D.E.W. is Irish character distilled down to the smoothest Irish whiskey around. It is quintessential Irish whiskey, combining all that is approachable yet complex about Ireland, its people and its whiskey.

The original Tullamore distillery was founded in 1829. The name of the whiskey is derived from the town in which it is made, Tullamore, Co. Offaly, and the initials of its founding father Daniel Edmund Williams (D.E.W.) who became the owner of the business in the 1890s and inspired the launch of world-famous Tullamore D.E.W. Irish Whiskey.

As the original triple blend of Irish whiskey, their three spirits come together to give a balance of flavour like no other in the category. The balance of grain, malt and pot still whiskeys brings outstanding quality and complexity to the liquid. By combining three spirits, this blend offers three dimensions of flavour to explore: fruit, spice and sweet.

The Tullamore D.E.W. award-winning range includes Tullamore D.E.W. original, XO Caribbean Rum Cask Finish, 12-Year-Old Special Reserve, 14-Year-Old Single Malt and 18-Year-Old Single Malt.

TRIPLE HOOK

A celebration of blending and the power of three – this three-ingredient cocktail is a nod to the Manhattan, a classic American whiskey cocktail, which allows to tie in the story of the bourbon casks. Fruity, cherry sweetness is ramped up by Maraschino liqueur and vermouth adds delicate spice. Enjoy at the end of the night, after dinner.

- *40ml Tullamore D.E.W. Original*
- *10ml Maraschino liqueur*
- *10ml vermouth*
- *1tsp elderflower liqueur*
- ***Garnish:*** *orange peel twist*

Add Tully, maraschino and vermouth to a mixing glass with quality ice and stir for 10 seconds. Strain into a cocktail glass and garnish with a fresh cut orange twist.

MICIL POITÍN

At Micil Distillery they craft exceptional spirits in tiny batches, using six generations of Connemara distilling heritage and experience. Their ambition has always been to produce the best quality spirits enriched by local Connemara ingredients. The craft has been passed down through the family for the last 170 years in Irish, which is still the spoken language at the distillery today.

Micil Mac Chearra began distilling in 1848 in Connemara. Six generations later Micil's direct descendant, Pádraic Ó Griallais, opened Galway's only distillery, having acquired the craft from his grandfather Jimmí. Today Pádraic and Micil Distillery represent the only continuous link to this unique Irish tradition.

Micil's smooth, spicy poitín became highly sought after in Connemara and often featured at parties, weddings and celebratory events in the west of Ireland. Their poitín has always been handcrafted and made entirely from quality grain. A Connemara flower called 'bogbean' is an ever-present ingredient, imparting a signature nutty flavour to the smooth, honey-tasting poitín.

MICIL SOUR

A Micil take on a classic sour made with poitín instead of whiskey. A fantastic must-try drink.

- *50ml Micil Poitín*
- *25ml lemon juice*
- *15ml sugar syrup*
- *3 dashes Angostura bitters*

Place all ingredients in a shaker with ice. Shake well and strain into a chilled glass with ice.

PENICILLIN

Another classic with a Micil twist. The original Penicillin recipe was created in New York in 2005. It may not be as effective as the antibiotic but the soothing flavours of honey, lemon and ginger will surely warm up a chilly winter night.

- *40ml Micil Poitín*
- *20ml lemon juice*
- *15ml honey*
- *2 pieces of fresh ginger*
- ***Garnish:*** *ginger slices*

Muddle ginger pieces in a shaker, add poitín, lemon juice and honey. Shake and strain into a glass with ice, float some poitín on top (about 10 ml) and garnish with ginger slices.

AROUND THE WORLD

Take a trip while at home. The flavours of coconut, lime and sweet spices will take you to a tropical place without having to leave your house. Sunshine in a glass.

- *50ml Micil Poitín*
- *50ml coconut milk*
- *2tsp natural yoghurt*
- *15ml sugar syrup*
- *Pinch of cinnamon*
- *1 vanilla pod, opened*
- **Garnish:** *star anise & lime zest*

Shake all ingredients with ice and fine strain into a glass. Garnish with star anise and grating of lime zest.

DINGLE GIN

Dingle Gin is the product of a considerable amount of technical and historical research, and of experimentation. In terms of its broad style, Dingle Gin is categorised as a London Dry Gin, but the unique character and flavour come from their painstaking and original choice of botanicals. A London Dry Gin is juniper-forward, at a minimum ABV of 37.5% and all elements of the gin (botanicals, alcohol etc.) are distilled. This combination of flavour elements is macerated in spirit for 24 hours. Then, when the spirit is distilled, it passes through a flavour basket in the neck of the still. This process underlines the attention to detail that is an essential part of the producers' whole approach to the art of distillation. They use a copper pot still to distil Dingle Gin. The copper pot still enhances the flavour of the gin while giving it a unique smoothness.

Rowan berry from mountain ash trees, fuchsia, bog myrtle, hawthorn and heather are used amongst other botanicals to give a taste of the Kerry landscape. It's a recipe unknown elsewhere and is gauged to create a sense of place and provenance. The spirit is collected at 70% ABV and then cut to 42.5% ABV using the purest of water drawn from their own well, 240 feet below the distillery. The spirit is then chill filtered in order to remove the fatty acids which can occur below 46% ABV. Dingle Gin is then hand-bottled on site and shipped all over the world.

Dingle Gin has received numerous accolades including Best Irish Gin in 2017 and in 2018 at the Irish Whiskey Awards, the award for World's Best London Dry Gin and the overall award for World's Best Gin at the 2019 World Gin Awards.

DINGLE ELDERFLOWER MARTINI

A slightly sweeter and flowery take on a classic Martini where elderflower syrup complements the botanical notes of Dingle Gin.

- *50ml Dingle Gin*
- *20ml Noilly Prat*
- *20ml elderflower syrup*
- **Garnish:** *orange peel twist*

Add all ingredients with orange peel to a shaker with plenty of ice and stir slowly to dissolve a lot of the ice cubes. Then double strain into a chilled glass. Garnish with an orange peel twist.

DINGLE BRAMBLE

A modern classic with a fruity flair. The cocktail was created in London in the 1980s and has been one of the most popular drinks ever since.

- *50ml Dingle Gin*
- *20ml lemon juice*
- *15ml Crème de Mûre*
- *10ml sugar syrup*
- ***Garnish:*** *blackberries*

Add all ingredients to a shaker, shake with ice and strain into a glass with crushed ice. Garnish with blackberries on a cocktail stick.

DINGLE GIN GIMLET

Sweet, sour, refreshing and easy on the palate, this cocktail is one of the best and most popular gin sours, with lime being the citrus of choice.

- *50ml Dingle Gin*
- *25ml lime syrup*
- *10ml fresh lime juice*
- ***Garnish:** lime wheel*

Shake all ingredients with ice and strain into a chilled martini glass. Garnish with a lime wheel.

CLONAKILTY WHISKEY

Clonakilty, on the coast of the southwestern tip of Ireland, is one of the most beautiful locations in the world and the Scully family has farmed this land for nine successive generations. Their mission is to create Clonakilty Whiskey using the best resources that nature has to offer: prime land, pristine water and salt sea air, the perfect ingredients for a maritime distillery.

The Scullys grow their own heritage barley on the family farm in the shadow of the Galley Head Lighthouse. Centuries of sea mist, soft rain and ocean spray provide a complexity to the soil that permeates through to each individual grain.

The state-of-the-art distillery is located a few short miles away in the heart of Clonakilty town, the three gleaming copper pot stills an inspiring sight to behold. The world's best new make single pot still is distilled here, an accolade awarded to Clonakilty Distillery at the World Whiskey Awards in 2020.

Pure clean air, transported across the thousands of miles of the Atlantic Ocean, provides a freshness unspoilt by human intervention and the Clonakilty Whiskey ocean warehouse, perched 200m above the sea, is ideal for maturing and finishing the finest of whiskeys. This is where the magic really happens, blending, ageing, bottling and hand-labelling. Casks are filled with Clonakilty Whiskey and left for the Irish salt sea air to work its magic. With a passion for innovation, Clonakilty Distillery strives to use only the best cask finishes for its whiskey including those in the current range: NEOC, Port, Bordeaux and Cognac casks.

Sustainability and environmental commitments are taken very seriously, and Clonakilty Distillery is a member of Bord Bia's Origin Green, an independently certified commitment to sustainable corporate practice. Additionally, the distillery is a proud sponsor of Whale and Dolphin Conservation, a global maritime conservation initiative.

So, when you receive a bottle of Clonakilty Whiskey you know it is something special. A spirit crafted by nature and kissed by the sea.

WINTER STORM

A take on the classic Old Fashioned with a Clonakilty twist. This premium Irish whiskey is matured in American oak and finished in port casks hence the aromas of sweet apples and fresh peaches, leading to flavours of cherries, raisins and soft spices.

- *60ml Clonakilty Port Cask Whiskey*
- *15ml demerara sugar syrup*
- *2 dashes Angostura bitters*
- *2 dashes cherry bitters*
- ***Garnish:** orange peel and cherry*

Pour the ingredients in a whiskey glass with a large ice cube. Garnish with an orange peel and cherry.

MAD MARCH HARE POITÍN

Poitín is making a huge comeback in Ireland. The poitín category predates that of Irish whiskey and for many years it was the drink of the Irish people.

Distilled using 100% malted barley, Mad March Hare is crafted in West Cork and is one of the true hidden gems you'll find in bars around Ireland with its creamy mouthfeel and ever-smooth finish. Mad March Hare poitín was awarded 'The Best Irish Poitín' at the Irish Whiskey Awards in 2019.

MAD MARCH MULE

The recipe comes from Bar 1661, Ireland's Best Bar of 2019 (Irish Craft Cocktail Awards). This cocktail is light and refreshing, perfect for drinking with friends and easy to batch.

- *30ml Mad March Hare Poitín*
- *2 dashes Angostura bitters*
- *1 dash orange water*
- *20ml lime juice*
- *15ml ginger syrup*
- *Hope Pale Ale*
- **Garnish:** *lime wedge*

Place all ingredients in a glass. Top with Hope Pale Ale. Garnish with a lime wedge.

Recipe by Dave Mulligan, Bar 1661, Dublin

KALAK VODKA

Kalak reflects and heightens the best parts of contemporary Ireland – simultaneously celebrating the ancient and the modern.

Kalak is a phonetic spelling of the Irish word 'cailleach' (meaning witch). Kalak is the embodiment of the darker, more powerful side of nature, and the side the producers harnessed to make their product. She was a Celtic deity, a goddess and the closest thing the Celts had to Mother Nature.

Kalak is the ancient earth herself. She is the lichen-covered rocks and the mountain peaks. She is the bare earth covered with snow and frost. She is the deep ancestress, veiled by the passage of time. Most importantly, she is the shadow side of Mother Nature and the Celtic queen of winter. She comes into power as the days shorten and the sun courses low in the skies.

The brand has been inspired by contemporary art and is proud of its heritage. 'We are compelled by our rich history in art, and its unique connection to nature.' Like many of the great Irish artists (Bacon, Yeats, Le Brocquy, Scully) who challenged convention by their elegant yet audacious interpretation of nature, space or the individual, the producers too, through Kalak, have endeavoured to create an Ireland 'as they see it'. This is an Ireland of paradoxes: old and new, raw and pure, nature and innovation.

The nature of art is echoed in the making of the vodka. It's this passion for creative excellence and hand-crafted precision that gives the brand a timeless sophistication.

Kalak is a vodka unlike any other, one with a new level of purity and smoothness that's there from the start – vodka with the cobwebs blown off.

As nature and the environment are the corner stones of its brand being, Kalak has passionately sourced all of its raw materials within the context of sustainable development. Whether it is the pureness of the ingredients, the eco-design bottle, the FSC certified labels, or the recyclable closures; Kalak is truly a protector of nature.

KALAK TIPPERARY

The classic Irish whiskey cocktail gets a contemporary Kalak twist. The creamy and biscuit notes in Kalak blend beautifully with the herbal Chartreuse and sweet vermouth.

- *35ml Kalak Vodka*
- *15ml green Chartreuse*
- *15ml sweet Italian vermouth*
- ***Garnish:*** *sprig of thyme studded with 3 green olives*

Pour all ingredients into a shaker with some ice. Stir for about 20 seconds and strain into a chilled tumbler. Stir the drink again for 10 seconds with the garnish. Fill the glass with ice and stir again.

BLACK BETTY

Discover the wicked and wild side of Kalak through Black Betty. She knows how to deliver a bittersweet smack of the most intense flavours.

- *50ml Kalak Vodka*
- *10ml Amaro Montenegro*
- *1tsp Irish blackcurrant jam*
- *10ml fresh lemon juice*
- *1 dash of Peychaud's bitters*
- *1 dash of orange bitters*
- **Garnish:** *orange peel twist*

Place all ingredients in a shaker and fill it with ice. Seal it and shake hard for 20 seconds. Fine strain into a chilled coupe glass. Garnish with an orange peel twist.

KALAK MARTINI

Wild Ireland meets urban chic in this elegant and sophisticated take on the classic Martini.

- *50ml Kalak Vodka*
- *Good dash of Lillet Blanc (5 or 10ml depending on your taste)*
- ***Garnish:*** *lemon peel twist*

Gently stir in a large glass with lots of ice, shake, then pour into a chilled martini glass. Garnish with a lemon peel twist.

GLENDALOUGH GIN

The Glendalough Distillery was set up by five friends from Wicklow and Dublin who shared a love of craft spirits. They eventually decided to leave the safety of their day jobs in Dublin and went into the mountains to take a chance on something more meaningful (much like the man on their bottle, St Kevin). Together they built a craft distillery near their favourite spot in those mountains where they produce whiskey, gin and poitín.

Glendalough (meaning The Valley of Two Lakes) is a glacial valley nestled in the Wicklow Mountains renowned for its early medieval monastic settlement founded in the 6th century by legendary monk St Kevin. Monasteries like Glendalough were the birthplace of distilled drinks and St Kevin is an eternal inspiration for the Glendalough team.

From the picturesque mountains, forests and fields surrounding the distillery, the Glendalough team forages fresh botanicals daily to encapsulate the taste of the valley in every bottle of gin produced. The use of Irish oak (just like the early settlement would have done) sustainably felled in forests surrounding the distillery has inspired some unique whiskey expressions to bring further flavours of Glendalough from their neck of the woods, to yours.

ROSE GIN SPRITZ

Rose Gin Spritz combines the floral and Turkish delight notes from Rose Gin with the fresh fruit juices and mint in a refreshing spritz with a naturally pink hue.

- *60ml Glendalough Rose Gin*
- *30ml sugar syrup*
- *30ml fresh lime juice*
- *30ml grapefruit juice*
- *soda water*
- **Garnish:** *grapefruit wheel & sprig of mint*

Shake with ice and strain. Top with soda water. Garnish with a grapefruit wheel and a freshly torn and slapped sprig of mint.

GINGLE BELLS

Dry, fruity and oh so festive. It'll spice up your holiday party and be a showstopper at a Christmas celebration. A perfect way to start the festive season.

- *50ml Glendalough Rose Gin*
- *25ml dry vermouth*
- *15ml lemon juice*
- *15ml cranberry syrup*
- *1 egg white*
- ***Garnish:*** *cranberry, rosemary sprig and pinch of cinnamon*

Shake all ingredients with ice. Strain into a chilled glass. Garnish with a cranberry, rosemary sprig and a pinch of cinnamon.

BERRY COLLINS

Tom Collins with a fruity twist. A perfect match of the rose gin and fruit makes it a simply fabulous summer cocktail.

- *50ml Glendalough Rose Gin*
- *25ml lemon juice*
- *25ml sugar syrup*
- *125ml soda water*
- *raspberries*
- **Garnish:** *lemon peel twist & raspberries*

Muddle a few raspberries in the bottom of a glass. Add ice and the remaining ingredients and mix well. Garnish with a lemon peel twist and a few raspberries.

EGAN'S WHISKEY

The Egan family has been involved in Irish Whiskey since the 1800s when Patrick and Henry Egan established general merchants P. & H. Egan Ltd in Tullamore, Co. Offaly. As entrepreneurs, the Egans were forward thinkers, showing remarkable innovation and agility in work practices for the time.

Today, they are working on the next chapter, bringing the taste of a modern and cosmopolitan Ireland to the world. They believe in making choices that push themselves forward, in following their convictions to create whiskeys with a taste profile that sets them apart.

Egan's Irish Whiskey, for extraordinary tastes.

EGAN'S FORTITUDE OLD FASHIONED

Egan's Fortitude recently won double gold and Irish Whiskey of the Year at the New York International Spirits Competition. Due to the maturation of Egan's Fortitude being aged purely in Pedro Ximenez Sherry Casks, this cocktail makes for an amazing twist on the classic Old Fashioned.

- *60ml Egan's Fortitude Whiskey*
- *1tsp demerara sugar*
- *4-5 dashes orange bitters*
- *1tsp water*
- ***Garnish:** orange zest & peel*

Muddle the sugar, water and orange bitters together until dissolved. Add Egan's Fortitude, ice and stir for 50-60 seconds. Strain into an old fashioned glass over a large ice cube and finish with an orange zest over the top. Garnish with an orange peel.

Recipe by: Ian Doody, former Beverage Director & Mixologist of The Rising Bar, Cambridge, Massachusetts

KILLOWEN POITÍN

A highly regarded recipe from a local Mourne family that was used for generations has now been reborn as a legal spirit. This allows it to be enjoyed by poitín and whiskey enthusiasts lucky enough to have a bottle.

Our geographically protected native spirit has enjoyed a recent revival in recent years. At Killowen, a unique ratio of wheat, barley and oats is carefully selected to create a mash bill fitting of the word poitín. Killowen Poitín is a substance of luxury created with skill and care.

This small batch produce is a celebration of Irish mash bill culture, and it includes mixes of malted and unmalted barley, oat, rye and wheat. Once regarded as an illicit highland produce, Killowen has vowed to restore poitín to its rightful place as an artisan spirit of choice by perfecting recipes using Ireland's only direct-fired stills and worm tub condensers. These methods are sadly long lost to modern efficiency and their revival adds complexity, viscosity and spice that resembles poitín pure pot still of old. Killowen Poitín honours real pot still and enables the consumer to taste the ancient Irish spirit and glimpse its imminent revival.

KILLOWEN OLD FASHIONED

A Killowen take on a classic Old Fashioned using poitín instead of whiskey. It's a real celebration of the nearly-forgotten white Irish spirit.

- *25ml Killowen Poitín*
- *1 sugar cube*
- *2 dashes Angostura bitters*
- *A few dashes plain water*
- **Garnish:** *orange slice, burnt*

Place the sugar cube in an old fashioned glass and saturate with bitters. Add a dash of plain water. Muddle until dissolved. Fill the glass with ice cubes and add whiskey. Garnish with freshly burnt orange slice.

CASK

Cask, located in Cork's beautiful Victorian Quarter, is a place like no other - stunning modern art deco design, excellent food and a seasonal farm-to-glass cocktail menu. The Cask team forages for wild ingredients and uses fantastic Irish-made spirits to create unique drinks that tell a story and push the boundaries of flavour and senses.

'At Cask we give our cocktail menu the same ethos that chefs in fine dining restaurants give their food menus,' said Andy Ferreira, the bar manager and award-winning mixologist. 'It's imperative you build a relationship with the ingredients and locality has to be at the forefront of everything we do. Cocktail menus were awash with everything from yuzu to coconut and the vast majority of spirits and modifiers used weren't produced in Ireland. We wanted to change that.'

Andy and his team, who are inspired by nature, set out to showcase the versatility of the native ingredients and base as many cocktails as they can around an Irish base spirit. They forged a rule that apart from the spirits, only ingredients that grew in Ireland would be used on their menus - no citrus or tropical fruit. Essentially anything imported is off the menu.

'What we've discovered over the last three-and-a-half years and 14 seasonal cocktail menus is there's a genuine passion and determination in the Irish drinks producing community that is contagious and is rightfully renowned the world over. More and more cocktail bars are starting to see the benefits of using Irish but we've undoubtably a long way to go,' said Andy.

Cask's philosophy - passion and the celebration of all things Irish - is admirable, inspiring and encouraging to support our local drinks industry and the amazing spirits it has to offer.

COOLE SWAN IRISH CREAM LIQUEUR

Based on the family farm in the heart of the Boyne Valley, Co. Meath, Coole Swan is the only Irish cream liqueur that combines single malt Irish whiskey, real Belgian white chocolate and fresh Irish cream. With all-natural ingredients, Coole Swan has a fresh, smooth, velvety, long-lasting, and creamy taste that lingers – a taste that took 213 attempts to get just right.

Inspired by tradition, created for now, the Irish cream liqueur is a distinctive indulgence. The unique name was inspired by *The Wild Swans at Coole*, a poem written by one of Ireland's great romantic poets - W.B. Yeats. In this poem Yeats writes of searching for an everlasting beauty in the world and Coole Swan was an effort to bottle that eternal elegance.

Coole Swan is consistently recognised as the multi-award-winning Irish cream liqueur. From New York to Nottingham and Dublin to Darwin, the Irish cream liqueur continues to grow and expand while never changing in its exquisite taste and dedication to quality ingredients. Crafted with love and passion. Made in Ireland and only in Ireland.

HIGH SOCIETY

Old fashioned grace and sophistication in the form of the High Society. The name is derived from the epitome of elegance, Grace Kelly, whose last film before becoming Princess of Monaco was called High Society. This cocktail possesses an incredibly smooth texture thanks to Coole Swan, and is bursting with harmonious flavours. The vanilla and rhubarb-infused gin pairs well with the tartness of fresh raspberries. This cocktail maintains the gorgeous cream colour of the Coole Swan with a very subtle pink hue from the gin and raspberries. Served over crushed ice, the High Society sits beautifully with a mint and raspberry garnish on top.

- *50ml Coole Swan*
- *20ml vanilla & rhubarb-infused gin*
- ***Garnish:*** *raspberries & mint*

Shake all ingredients with ice. Strain into a martini glass slowly. Garnish with raspberries and mint.

THE BLACK PEARL

A cocktail inspired by the adventurous pirates of the Caribbean Sea. The combination of the velvety Irish Cream Liqueur and the warm Caribbean spiced rum is unexpected but perfect. The Blue Curacao enhances the orange and caramel notes of the spiced rum. With the addition of the Blue Curacao, The Black Pearl has a very fun and eye-catching blue colour which is reminiscent of the seas sailed by the pirates.

- *50ml Coole Swan*
- *25ml premium spiced rum*
- *10ml Blue Curacao*
- ***Garnish:** blackberries*

Add all ingredients into a shaker with lots of ice, shake vigorously and pour into a martini glass. Garnish with blackberries.

COOLE SWAN ESPRESSO MARTINI

The Espresso Martini has a fairly recent history compared to many other cocktails. It was created in the early 1980s by Dick Bradsel and has since skyrocketed in popularity. The Coole Swan Espresso Martini looks just as dramatic as the classic Espresso Martini, however, upon closer inspection the foam top is replaced with the velvety smooth Irish Cream Liqueur.

- *75-100ml Coole Swan*
- *25ml vodka*
- *75ml coffee liqueur*

Put the coffee liqueur and the vodka into a shaker full of ice and shake for 10-15 seconds. Pour into a cocktail glass. Pour the Coole Swan on top of the coffee mix over the back of a spoon to create a layer.

MUFF GIN

'Tradition is an important part of who we are as people. We want to believe that the things we buy were crafted with a skill and a love that spans generations, that each individual iteration of the product carries something unique and that it will bring us back to a place we know is special. This idea of tradition is key to the identity of The Muff Liquor Company.'

Donegal is a wild and wonderful place on the most northwesterly point of Ireland and the peninsula of Inishowen is where the story of The Muff Liquor Company begins.

In the early 20th century, Philip McClenaghan grew potatoes in the fields around Greencastle, Inishowen. He started experimenting with a potion made exclusively of potatoes and spent many hours perfecting his creation.

Philip McClenaghan remained part of the fabric of village life up until his later years, by which stage he had passed down his stories and secrets to a new generation. His granddaughter Laura, daughter of Mary, now continues his storied tradition of making a product born of the land and crafted by hand. Her ambition is to make sure The Muff Liquor Company is a testament to the hardworking values of her grandad Philip McClenaghan. His secret to a long life? "Plenty of hard work" - although a healthy dash of his finely crafted spirit did no harm either.

THE MUFF MAN

A refreshing cocktail where citrus and herb notes of the lime and mint are rounded out by the sweetness of the elderflower.

- *50ml Muff Gin*
- *25ml elderflower syrup*
- *25ml lime juice*
- *4-5 mint leaves*
- *Tonic water*
- ***Garnish:** lime wheel & sprig of rosemary*

Place all ingredients in a glass. Top with a splash of tonic. Garnish with a lime wheel and a sprig of rosemary.

TEELING WHISKEY

Right in the heart of the Liberties, against the backdrop of a city steeped in whiskey history, the Teeling Whiskey Distillery opened its doors in 2015 as the first new distillery in Dublin for over 125 years.

Teeling is a new generation of Dublin distillers who approach their craft with a respect for generations passed and with the confidence to forge the next chapter. Here at the home of the Spirit of Dublin, the liquid tells the story.

Since Jack and Stephen Teeling founded the company in 2012, Teeling Whiskey has become the leader of the new generation of Irish whiskey companies, winning more than 300 international awards for its unique whiskey expressions.

Irish whiskey is smooth and approachable by nature. The unique temperate climate doesn't reach the sweltering peaks of Kentucky heat, or the icy lows of the Scottish Highlands. This means little variation in temperature occurs during ageing, producing Irish whiskey's signature mellow taste.

'Building on this approachable base we experiment at all stages of the process. From the malting and blending of grains to the yeast used in the fermentation and the distillation process itself, we dare to be different. If distilling is a science, the processes of barrel selection, ageing and blending is a craft perfected by human palates and noses. The delicate base of Irish whiskey is the perfect canvas upon which to layer character, flavour and depth. Varying the time, style and number of barrels at this stage adds the subtlety and complexity of flavour we pride ourselves on.'

The Teeling Small Batch Irish Whiskey, their flagship whiskey, challenges the convention of what an Irish whiskey can be, with layers of unique flavour influenced by unconventional cask maturation techniques. Hand-selected casks of grain and malt whiskey are initially fully aged in former bourbon barrels, then married together in Central American rum casks for up to 12 months for a unique, dried fruit profile.

TROPICAL TEELING

Sometimes a long drink is precisely what you would prefer, something to sip on over a while, where the whiskey is lengthened with a complementary mixer. Rum influenced Teeling Irish Whiskey and home-made pineapple soda, lovely and refreshing with natural character bursting with fruit forward flavours and a bright effervescence.

- *40ml Teeling Small Batch Whiskey*
- *20ml pineapple syrup*
- *100ml soda water*
- ***Garnish:** fresh lime wedge & sprig of mint*

Put all ingredients in a tall glass with cubed ice and stir. Garnish with a wedge of lime and a sprig of mint.

NEW (MARKET) FASHIONED

The Old Fashioned cocktail, arguably one of the most famous original cocktails is currently seeing a huge resurgence in popularity. Having seen many variations over the years with many different whiskeys, this modern version takes inspiration from, and is built around, the flavours of the award-winning rum-influenced Teeling Small Batch. Highlighting the unique flavours within of dried fruits and spice while not veering too far from what makes this cocktail a true classic.

- *50ml Teeling Small Batch Whiskey*
- *10ml spiced rum*
- *10ml honey syrup*
- *2 dashes Angostura Bitters*
- ***Garnish:*** *orange peel*

Add all ingredients to a stirring glass. Stir well with ice and strain over fresh cubed ice into a whiskey glass. Garnish with a twist of orange peel.

TEELING IRISH COFFEE

Invented in Ireland, popularised in San Francisco, there are few people in the world that have not had the opportunity to try, or at the very least heard of, an incarnation of the world-famous Irish Coffee cocktail. Easily one of the best-selling cocktails at the Teeling Distillery, sometimes you only get one opportunity to make an impact with Irish whiskey cocktails and to stress the importance of serving the most amazing memorable Teeling Irish Coffee each and every time.

- *40ml Teeling Small Batch Whiskey*
- *120ml freshly brewed filter coffee*
- *20ml demerara sugar syrup*
- *Double cream*
- ***Garnish:*** *grated nutmeg*

Preheat your coffee glass with hot water. Empty the glass. Add the whiskey, coffee and syrup. Top with double cream using the back of a spoon. Garnish with grated nutmeg.

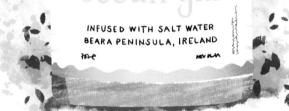

beara

ocean gin

INFUSED WITH SALT WATER
BEARA PENINSULA, IRELAND

BEARA GIN

Inspired by the beauty of their birthplace - the Beara Peninsula - and passionate about all things gin, siblings- John and Eileen embarked on a voyage of discovery to create their own signature gin. They spent 18 months travelling around the world meeting distillers and gin enthusiasts to learn as much as possible about this enigmatic spirit. They enrolled in gin school to learn the craft of distilling and blending.

They wanted to create a spirit that reflected the natural beauty of their homeplace and their love of the sea. And so, Beara Ocean Gin was born – a hand-crafted, small batch gin, infused with wild Atlantic sea water and Ventry harbour sugar kelp. Hand-picked fuchsia – the iconic flower of West Cork – is combined with traditional gin botanicals to create a well-balanced easy-drinking gin.

The installation of the modern iStill and traditional Müller gin still were landmark moments for the team. Under the guidance of Frank Deiter, they experimented with the new stills, tested gin recipes and tweaked processes to create a gin as impressive as the surrounding landscape.

A final recipe was created and the team started to produce, bottle and package Beara Ocean Gin. The company joined the SuperValu Retail Academy programme and progressed through the stages to supply a number of stores in the Cork/Kerry region. Beara Distillery partnered with a number of key distributors to grow its reach and supply bars and restaurants. The distillery continues to grow and fulfil its mission to provide customers with a refreshing taste of West Cork, wherever they may be.

BEES KNEES

This is a take on the classic 1920s prohibition era cocktail. Honey and lemon were added to mask the taste and smell of bathtub gin.

- *20ml Beara Ocean Gin*
- *40ml Kinsale Atlantic Dry Mead*
- *10ml honey syrup*
- *10ml fresh lemon juice*
- ***Garnish:*** *lemon peel*

Place all ingredients in a shaker. Shake well and pour in a saucer cocktail glass with a lemon twist to garnish.

Recipe by Tom, Milo and Jean at The Supper Club, Kinsale

GIZ A BEARA DAH

A refreshing cocktail packed full of flavour and aroma. A perfect summertime drink best enjoyed al fresco.

- *40ml Beara Ocean Gin*
- *20ml rosemary syrup*
- *20ml lemon juice*
- *1 egg white*
- *Light beer*

Shake first four ingredients with ice. Pour into a glass with ice. Top up with beer.

BEARA 100

A stylish and exciting celebratory drink and a great warm weather sipper. A perfect choice for a summer get together.

- *30ml Beara Ocean Gin*
- *10ml lemon juice*
- *20ml cardamom syrup with seaweed and lemongrass tea*
- *1 egg white*
- *Prosecco*
- **Garnish:** *lemon peel*

Shake first four ingredients with ice. Strain into a Champagne flute. Top up with Prosecco. Garnish with a lemon twist.

BÁN POITÍN

Bán Poitín was created in 2012 by a London-based, Irish bartender Dave Mulligan in his Irish-focused speakeasy, *Shebeen*. Starting as a passion project he quickly introduced his illicit Irish spirit to the London on-trade with a focus on educating the category, not the brand. It is this approach that has seen Mulligan establish himself as one of the leading ambassadors in poitín's revival. With cocktail listings in some of the city's most revered cocktail bars, Bán Poitín has firmly cemented itself in Ireland's cocktail culture.

Dave Mulligan has since opened one of Ireland's most exciting new venues, Bar 1661 which won 'Ireland's Best Cocktail Bar' 2019, on Dublin's historic north side. Once again giving a platform to promote the category Mulligan continues to use Bán Poitín as an education piece to inspire the next generation of Irish bartenders to embrace a nearly-forgotten piece of Irish culture.

Produced and bottled by The Echlinville Distillery in Co. Down, Bán Poitín was awarded Ireland's Best Poitín at the Irish Whiskey Awards for an unrivalled three years in a row. Made from barley grown and malted at the distillery, the addition of potato and molasses makes the spirit unique. Bottled at 48%, Bán is a brand that stays true to poitín's notorious reputation as a full-flavoured statement of origin. A Barrelled and Buried series has seen Bán explore American, Islay and Spanish oak barrels as well as a bottled version of its signature Belfast Coffee cocktail.

BELFAST COFFEE

Belfast Coffee is a cold brewed twist on the popular Irish Coffee using poitín instead of whiskey.

- *30ml Bán Poitín*
- *60ml cold brew coffee*
- *15ml demerara sugar syrup*
- *Double cream*
- ***Garnish:*** *fresh nutmeg*

Stir the poitín, cold brew and sugar syrup over ice. Strain into an Irish Coffee glass. Float a finger of thickened double cream. Garnish with grated fresh nutmeg.

Recipe by Dave Mulligan, Bar 1661, Dublin.

LONGUEVILLE HOUSE IRISH APPLE BRANDY

The origin of Longueville House's Irish Apple Brandy goes back many centuries to the Celts, who worshipped the apple tree as a symbol of fertility. They brought it with them when they migrated to Ireland through Spain (Asturias), France (Calvados), England (Somerset) and Wales.

Apples have been grown in the Blackwater Valley for a very long time, as is evident from old Irish local names such as Balinahulla and Ballyhooly, the Irish for apple is úl.

At Longueville House, there is a field beside the Big Wood known as Orchard Field, whose name predates the earliest records of the 17th century. So perhaps it was destiny that led current owner's father, Michael, to plant a substantial orchard in the demesne 25 years ago.

Historically, Ireland was a country full of small breweries and distilleries before the advent of the train in the 19th century and the motor car in the 20th century. (And, today, we think we have invented the concept of buying local!) As transport improved, gradually the bigger players we know today started to take over – a process accelerated by successive governments' tax-raising policies, along with a Church that increasingly demonised the consumption of alcohol.

The earliest recorded reference to the distillation of cider is in 1774 and is included in a guide to the city and county of Cork.

Longueville House Irish Apple Brandy won Georgina Campbell's Natural Food Award in 2014 as well as the Gold Medal Award at the Irish Food and Drinks Awards/Blas Na hEireann in 2013, 2014 and 2015. It is the only Irish Spirit to have ever won gold three years in a row at Blas na hEireann beating Irish whiskeys.

SUGAR & SPICE

Get in the Christmas spirit and impress your guests with this sweet and spicy festive cocktail. Spread some holiday magic with Sugar & Spice.

- *30ml Longueville House Apple Brandy*
- *25ml port*
- *15ml thyme & cinnamon syrup*
- *20ml lemon juice*
- **Garnish:** *sprig of thyme*

Shake all ingredients with ice. Strain into a coupe glass and garnish with a sprig of thyme.

Recipe by Darren Hogarty & Ross Lewis of Chapter One, Dublin.

DAN DUGGAN

Named after head cider maker and distiller at the Longueville House, this rich and aromatic hot drink is a hug in a tea cup. Sit by the fire and enjoy the incredible fusion of flavours.

- *45ml Longueville House Apple Brandy*
- *15ml Buckfast tonic wine*
- *25ml Beamish (or other Stout)*
- *15ml seasonal cordial of your choice*
- *50ml boiling water*

Heat the ingredients in a small pot. Pour into a tea cup and serve with a digestive biscuit.

Recipe by Andy Ferreira of Cask, Cork

PADDY THE FARMER

This robust and earthy cocktail is a pure celebration of Irishness. Apple brandy, whiskey and ginger beer complement each other while lemon and mint bring out the refreshing aromas.

- *20ml Longueville House Apple Brandy*
- *30ml Irish whiskey*
- *15ml lemon juice*
- *5ml sugar syrup*
- *Ginger beer*
- **Garnish:** *sprig of mint*

Add first four ingredients in a shaker. Shake with ice and strain into a highball glass over ice. Top with ginger beer and garnish with a mint sprig.

THE SEXTON WHISKEY

An unexpected single malt made for restless and defiant spirits who challenge themselves to make choices every day, that add up to a life story worth telling. The Sexton is rich in hue, bold in taste and memorable in character.

The word Sexton is derived from medieval Latin, meaning the custodian of sacred objects or precious things. Similarly, master blender Alex Thomas is the caretaker of this unique Irish single malt while it rests in the casks, born out of intense experimentation and awaiting its next Sexton – the whiskey drinker.

The Sexton Single Malt is made with a respect for tradition and a passion for innovation: a true single malt distilled entirely from Irish malted barley and then triple distilled in copper pot stills before it is matured in Oloroso Sherry casks. The liquid represents the changing face of Ireland – capturing the provenance of the past and the optimism of the future.

Crafted with a versatile flavour profile, mix it, drink it with ice, drink it neat.

BURY THE HATCHET

This refreshing Bury the Hatchet whiskey cocktail oozes a bold flavour that you won't forget. The lemon juice enhances the complex citrus notes of The Sexton Single Malt, while the hint of sugar complements the smooth honey finish of the spirit.

- *50ml The Sexton Single Malt*
- *25ml lemon juice*
- *12.5ml sugar syrup*
- *Soda water*
- *15ml Pedro Ximénez*
- ***Garnish:*** *lemon peel twist*

Pour the whiskey into a tall glass over cubed ice. Add the lemon juice and sugar syrup. Top with soda water and a Pedro Ximenez float. Garnish with a twist of lemon.

MÓR GIN

Inspired by a tale of relentless adventure and a legacy, Mór is a bold and innovative gin made out of Arderin Distillery, a craft gin distillery founded by Eoin Bara in 2015 and located in Tullamore, Co. Offaly. It is the product of a legacy stretching back to the 1930s when his grandfather was a master distiller of world-renowned Irish whiskey.

In his youth, Eoin was enthralled by his grandfather's stories of a world where crafting a premium quality spirit wasn't something you just did but was an expression of who you were as a person. Eoin travelled the world to refine and perfect the techniques he learned and now he has created a gin that is an expression of who he is and an homage to the legacy his grandfather created.

Mór is much more than just a good gin, it's a celebration of a bygone era blended expertly with the secrets of generations of skilled craftsmen to produce a quality spirit that will stand the test of time.

FRENCH 75

This classic favourite is named after the French 75mm light field gun which was used by the French army in the First World War and later on became a symbol of hope in the battle against Germany. It is now one of the most loved cocktails ever created.

- *30ml Mór Irish Gin*
- *15ml lemon juice*
- *15ml sugar syrup*
- *90ml Champagne*
- **Garnish:** *lemon peel twist*

Shake first three ingredients with ice. Strain into a Champagne flute. Top up with Champagne. Garnish with a lemon peel twist.

LITTLE MISS SUNSHINE

This excellent aperitif cocktail combines the aromatic subtlety of gin with the bitter orange tang of Aperol. Refreshing, easy to make and simply delicious.

- *30ml Mór Irish Gin*
- *20ml Aperol*
- *20ml lemon juice*
- *20ml sugar syrup*
- *100ml tonic water*
- ***Garnish:** orange wedge*

Shake first four ingredients with ice. Strain into a wine glass. Top up with tonic water. Garnish with an orange wedge.

RED-HAIRED MARY

Light and herbal with the lavender and perfectly citrusy with the lemon, this cocktail is sweet, floral and beautifully refreshing. An ideal celebratory concoction.

- *40ml Mór Irish Gin*
- *20ml lemon juice*
- *20ml lavender liqueur*
- *75ml Rosé Cava Brut*
- *Soda water*
- ***Garnish:*** *rose petal*

Shake first three ingredients with ice. Strain into a wine glass. Top up with cava and soda water. Garnish with a rose petal.

KINSALE MEAD

Kate and Denis set up Kinsale Mead Co. in 2016 with a vision and passion to rediscover the art of mead-making and create a world-class range of Irish meads. Their family-run meadery in West Cork is Ireland's first meadery in almost 200 years.

Mead, also known as 'honey wine', is believed to be the world's oldest alcoholic drink, dating back to 6,000 BC and has a rich and colourful history in Ireland.

In order to create their award-winning meads, Kate and Denis researched traditional recipes and mead styles and applied the best wine-making techniques, coupled with a careful selection of raw honey, fruits and yeast.

Their range is handcrafted and made in small batches from bee to bottle in Kinsale, Co. Cork. With a close eye on sustainability and Bord Bia Origin Green certified, they develop and produce meads which embody the modern, refined style of mead-making.

Their meads are multiple gold medal winners at the Blas na hEireann Irish Food Awards, the Great Taste Awards (UK) and at the Mazer Cup in the USA.

Their entertaining and popular tours at the meadery are a great way to discover the history, craft and taste of this versatile drink. Their visitor experience won a TripAdvisor Travellers' Choice Award in 2020.

WILD RED STORM

Kinsale Meads are finished off dry and sit somewhere in between dry vermouth and applejack or calvados. You can utilise both sweetness and bitterness from mead to create refreshingly different delicious cocktails. The Wild Red Storm uses Kinsale Wild Red Mead, a berry mead made from Wexford blackcurrants beautifully balanced with dark sweet cherries, tempered over a hint of honey and matured to a very smooth finish.

- *40ml Wild Red Mead*
- *40ml ginger beer*
- ***Garnish:*** *blueberries & lime wheel*

Shake Wild Red Mead and ginger beer with ice. Pour into a tall glass over ice. Garnish with blueberries and a lime wheel.

MEADERITA

This cocktail is sharp and salty like an acerbic South-Western pirate.

- *40ml Atlantic Dry Mead*
- *20ml gold tequila*
- *20ml fresh lime juice*
- **Garnish:** *lime wheel*

Shake the mead, tequila and lime juice with ice. Salt the rim of a margarita glass. Pour into the glass and garnish with a lime wheel.

MULLED MEAD

A warming festive drink for cold winter days. Heat in a pan in the kitchen and soon the whole house will be filled with the lovely aromas.

- *1 bottle of Wild Red Mead*
- *1 cinnamon stick*
- *Piece of star anise*
- *2tsp of honey*
- *Orange peel*

In a saucepan, warm all ingredients gently. Do not boil. Serve in a heatproof glass or a mug.

BAR 1661

Award-winning Bar 1661 on Dublin's historic north side specialises in Irish spirits - poitín in particular - and showcases the great products Ireland has to offer. The bar was named after the year poitín was banned on the island.

Dave Mulligan, the owner of the bar and his own poitín brand, Bán Poitín, thinks there is a huge appetite for this category in Ireland. His aspiration is to get people enthusiastic and appreciative of the nearly forgotten Irish white spirit - an important part of Irish history and culture.

'Craft cocktail culture is still in its infancy in Ireland and we have a long way to go. With huge start-up costs we have a massive barrier to entry for independent bars resulting in a lack of experiential or experimental venues,' said Dave.

'While we have an exciting amount of craft distilleries popping up all over the island, the corporate structure of many bar companies and their suppliers threatens to stifle any home success these producers may have with imported and mass produced brand.'

Dave's passion and dedication is inspiring and his words only show how important it is to support and promote Irish craft spirit makers.

In 2019, Bar 1661 won 'Ireland's Best Cocktail Bar' at the Irish Craft Cocktail Awards.

Venues including Cask in Cork, The Sitting Room at The Delahunt in Dublin and his own team of bartenders at Bar 1661 will continue to inspire Dave to change drinks culture in Ireland for the better.

BLACKS GOLDEN RUM

Blacks Brewery was born out of passion by founders, Sam and Maudeline Black. What started as a hobby for the husband and wife team quickly became an obsession and led to a desire to experiment and create with enthusiasm and drive.

In 2015 they expanded and added a distillery, where a range of boutique spirits including gin, rum and whiskey are produced. This crossover between brewery and distillery is unique and gives them the option to age their beers in spirit barrels and vice versa to improve the depth of flavour.

In 2018 Blacks Distillery made history by producing Ireland's first-ever rum, distilled from start to finish at their home in Kinsale. Using only the finest sugar cane molasses, their rum has since been recognised on a global scale, winning gold at the World Rum Awards in 2020.

'We pride ourselves on our innovative approach to distilling, ignoring the mainstream trends and creating our own unique range of spirits, using quality ingredients and quirky flavour combinations.'

The award-winning Blacks Golden Rum is an incredibly robust golden rum characterised by the finest single malt Irish whiskey barrels in which they were matured. These are the very same barrels which first aged their 12-year-old Blacks Irish Whiskey.

On the nose you are transported to a dessert lovers' heaven with aromas of butterscotch sauce, banoffee pie and vanilla maple syrup, teamed with underlying layers of candied fruit. The smooth, rich toffee rum is velvet soft on the palate, boasting flavours of antique mahogany, caramel coated nuts and a fruity light to medium body.

THE FASHIONABLE PIRATE

Simple but sophisticated. It'll stretch your imagination and take you all the way to the Caribbean!

- *60ml Blacks Golden Rum*
- *2 dashes Angostura bitters*
- *10ml water*
- *10ml sugar syrup*
- ***Garnish:*** *orange peel*

Stir well with ice for 20 seconds. Strain and serve over a large ice cube. Garnish with an orange peel.

APPLE PIE

Autumn in a glass. Sweet and spicy notes from apple and cinnamon work really well with the golden rum making it a perfect fall concoction.

- *20ml Blacks Golden Rum*
- *10ml cinnamon liqueur*
- *5ml demerara sugar syrup*
- *5ml lemon juice*
- *20ml apple cider*
- ***Garnish:** dried apple slice*

Shake first four ingredients with ice. Strain into a glass with ice. Top with apple cider. Garnish with a dried apple slice.

JUNGLE PUNCH

Tropical sweetness at its finest. Fun and easy to make. Best enjoyed with family and friends at a garden party.

- *30ml Blacks Golden Rum*
- *10ml Campari*
- *20ml pineapple juice*
- *10ml lime syrup*
- ***Garnish:*** *pineapple wedge & leaf*

Shake all ingredients with ice. Strain into a glass with ice. Garnish with a pineapple wedge and a pineapple leaf.

W.D. O'CONNELL WHISKEY

O'Connell Whiskey Merchants is a family-owned whiskey company that procures premium new make spirit and aged whiskeys from multiple distilleries. They apply their own maturation and finish preferences by sourcing casks from a personal network of vineyards, bodegas and cooperages in Europe and the United States. Sourcing from multiple distilleries and using a strict wood management policy that reflects upon the history of Irish whiskey through the ages they are building a library of whiskey flavours.

This brand curates exceptional Irish whiskeys, matured and finished in interesting ways for whiskey lovers looking for something alternative yet timeless. A focus on transparency led the whole design process with every aspect of the branding and packaging telling an authentic story.

The Bill Phil is a triple-distilled peated single malt, the first in Ireland in over a century and gets its name from the southwest of Ireland. There were many different O'Connells in the village and its surrounds, and so nicknames were needed to avoid confusion. Daithí's great-grandfather, William Phillip, and his family became known as the Bill Phil O'Connells. Bill Phil was a blacksmith, farmer and merchant storekeeper known for forging peat-cutting tools and so, when they created this peated Irish whiskey it was naturally called the Bill Phil.

THE PX series: first up was a 17-year-old finished in Pedro Ximénez sherry casks. These are casks that were commonly seen in Ireland throughout the 1800s and this series represents the links with historical bonding and maturation of whiskey from that era.

BOULEVARD

The bittersweet Boulevard was devised to highlight lemon-scented smoke of Bill Phil through a riff on a classic Boulevardier by Harry McElhone.

- *20ml Bill Phil Whiskey*
- *20ml vermouth*
- *20ml Campari*
- *3 dashes citrus bitters*
- ***Garnish:*** *lemon peel twist*

Place all ingredients in a mixing glass. Serve over block ice in an old fashioned glass with lemon oils expressed over top. Garnish with a lemon peel twist.

BILL PHIL & GINGER

An alternative, less sweet version of a classic Whiskey & Ginger where the whiskey is still at the fore.

- *50ml Bill Phil Whiskey*
- *15ml ginger syrup*
- *20ml fresh lemon juice*
- *100ml soda water*
- **Garnish:** *lemon peel twist*

Shake first three ingredients with ice and strain into a tall chilled Collins glass with ice. Top with chilled soda, lightly stirring to incorporate. Express lemon oils over top. Garnish with a lemon peel twist.

LE MAILLOT VERT

Earthy, zesty and smokey yet sweet and warm. An exciting marriage of flavours and aromas.

- *40ml Bill Phil Whiskey*
- *20ml green Chartreuse*
- *15ml Fino Sherry*
- *20ml ginger extract*
- *20ml lime juice*
- *20ml burnt sugar syrup*
- *3 drops hedgerow bitters (Off The Cuff)*
- *40ml tonic water*
- **Garnish:** *lime grass & citrus mist*

Shake and strain over crushed ice. Top with tonic water. Garnish with lime grass and citrus mist.

HA'PENNY GIN

The Ha'penny range of handcrafted, small batch distilled spirits captures the flavours, stories and charm of Dublin and is as original and unforgettable as the city that inspired it.

For Dublin is a city of character and of characters and is warm, witty and welcoming in equal measure. And that spirit has connected people through the years, just as the Ha'penny Bridge joined the people of Dublin.

The range was created by craft enthusiasts at the Pearse Lyons Distillery at St James, who were inspired by the iconic Ha'penny Bridge which is recognised throughout the world as a symbol of this inimitable and charismatic city.

Ha'penny Rhubarb Gin is a refreshing, distinctively pink small batch pot distilled gin featuring the finest rhubarb alongside 13 expertly selected botanicals. The Ha'penny range features geranium, dandelion, lavender and blackberry, botanicals which grew in the nearby Phoenix Park in Victorian times when the bridge was built.

HA'PENNY RHUBARB SOUR

A Ha'penny take on a classic sour, this cocktail is a perfect balance of lemon, gin and syrup. The rhubarb gives the drink an exciting twist and a stunning pink hue.

- *50ml Ha'penny Rhubarb Gin*
- *30ml lemon juice*
- *20ml sugar syrup*
- *1 egg white*
- *3 dashes Angostura bitters*

Place all ingredients in a cocktail shaker. Shake vigorously for 20 seconds. Open the shaker and fill with ice. Shake again for another 20 seconds. Pour into a small coupe glass through a fine strainer. To finish, add the bitters on the foam close together and pull a cocktail stick through the foam.

WEST CORK WHISKEY

It has often been said about West Cork Distillers that it is a place built for and run by the people, for the people. Based in Skibbereen, West Cork Distillers was founded in 2003 by John O'Connell, Denis (Den) McCarthy and Ger McCarthy and has since grown to a team of more than 100 people.

It all started out in a room at the back of Den's house in 2003, at a time when it made very little economic sense to produce whiskey.

The early years were far from glamorous. One of their earlier products, the low ABV Kennedy range targeted at the Asian market, was heavily criticised by whiskey connoisseurs. Meanwhile, their first product, Drombeg, caught the attention of the tax authorities, but in true West Cork style, they represented themselves in fighting their case... and won!

Unperturbed by external factors and public opinion, the lads worked tirelessly to make West Cork Distillers a success. Hard graft was second nature to them, considering their previous roles in the fishing industry and John's R&D role in Kerry Group.

In 2014 they moved into a new distillery on Market Street in Skibbereen, with the Rocket still being described as 'the fastest still in the world' by drinks consultants Joel Harrison and Neil Ridley.

Fast forward to today, and the distillery operates out of a 12-acre area on Marsh Road, Skibbereen. Its core West Cork whiskey has won numerous awards, is for sale in more than 70 countries and is matured, distilled and bottled for some of the largest retailers and well-known personalities in the country.

West Cork has a proud history of artisan food and beverage production. West Cork Distillers is committed to upholding this reputation and to providing sustainable employment to the unspoiled part of the world they call home.

EMERALD

Named after the Emerald Isle, it's an Irish version of a classic Manhattan. Elegant and smooth with the notes of dried fruit and soft spices. A cocktail made for sipping by the fire.

- *60ml West Cork Whiskey*
- *30ml red vermouth*
- *1 dash orange bitters*
- ***Garnish:*** *orange peel*

Stir well with cracked ice, then strain into a chilled cocktail glass. Garnish with an orange peel.

PEARSE WHISKEY

Founded by Dundalk-born Pearse Lyons, The Pearse Lyons Distillery at St James was born out of a personal passion for brewing and distilling, an entrepreneurial spirit and a deep-rooted family connection with The Liberties.

The boutique distillery features two unique copper stills, nestled in the sanctuary of the restored historic St James' Church. These stills produce a range of small batch craft whiskeys which are aged in a superior ex-bourbon casks.

The team of four full-time distillers is led by head distiller, Gearoid Cahill – a veteran of the Irish drinks industry – and the product pipeline is inspired by global whiskey ambassador Conor Ryan, a renowned spirits enthusiast and mixologist.

Descending from six generations of coopers, Pearse Lyons' ancestry is steeped in the traditions and heritage of Irish brewing and distilling. A trailblazer in the drinks industry, Pearse was the first Irishman to receive a formal degree in brewing and distilling from the British School of Malting and Brewing and he counts Harp Brewery, Guinness and Irish Distillers among his early employers.

Following the completion of a PhD in yeast fermentation, Pearse moved to the US where he founded Alltech, a global biotechnology business with yeast at its core. His deep connection with the art of brewing and distilling never left him and in 1999 he acquired the oldest craft brewery in Lexington which is now home to Town Branch Distillery.

The story of the Pearse Lyons Distillery at St James began in 2011 when Pearse, keen to revisit his roots, sourced two magnificent signature pot stills and transported them to Ireland to begin distilling Irish whiskey. Following an extensive refurbishment of St James Church in Dublin's historic 'Golden Triangle' whiskey district, the Pearse Lyons Distillery at St James opened its doors in 2017.

Pearse Distillers Choice is a malt and grain whiskey blend aged in a combination of former bourbon and sherry barrels for a minimum of seven years.

LIBERTIES MANHATTAN

The original Manhattan recipe is believed to date back to the late 1800s. Bitters are a must, and bring the whiskey and vermouth together in this timeless and classy cocktail.

- *50ml Pearse Whiskey (7 year old)*
- *20ml red vermouth*
- *10ml white vermouth*
- *1 dash Angostura bitters*
- *1 dash Peychauds bitters*
- ***Garnish:** orange peel*

Put all ingredients into a mixing glass with large pieces of ice. Stir until chilled and pour into a cocktail glass. Spritz and garnish with an orange peel.

AQUA VITAE

Aqua Vitae is a new spirit based on the first written record of distillation in medieval Ireland which was created by Richard De Ledrede, the Bishop of Ossory, in Kilkenny circa 1324. After painstaking research, Chris Hennessy and Jarrod Cuffe used the original recipe to recreate the Aqua Vitae we have today.

First intended as an internal and topical cure-all, Aqua Vitae is both the origin and precursor to poitín, uisce beatha and whiskey as we know it. Its rich use of botanicals for medicinal components also makes it an ancestor of bitters.

Chris Hennessy, a Kilkenny native, is head bartender of The Dylan Whisky Bar and whiskey ambassador of the Kilkenny Whiskey Guild. He has been fascinated by the Aqua Vitae recipe since he first read about it in Fionnán O'Connor's book *A Glass Apart.*

Jarrod Cuffe is the founder of Off the Cuffe, which specialises in making bitters from organic botanicals macerated in new make Irish whiskey (whiskey before it has gone into barrel). Off the Cuffe bitter solutions is based in the Chocolate Factory, Dublin.

THE ORIGINAL
14TH CENTURY
RECIPE

AQUA VITAE

BISHOP OF OSSORY
RICHARD DE LEDREDE
KILKENNY

FOR WHOM THE BELL TOLLS

"There is nothing else than now. There is neither yesterday, certainly, nor is there any tomorrow. How old must you be before you know that? There is only now, and if now is only two days, then two days is your life and everything in it will be in proportion. This is how you live a life in two days. And if you stop complaining and asking for what you never will get, you will have a good life. A good life is not measured by any biblical span." Hemingway, 1940.

- *45ml Aqua Vitae*
- *20ml fresh lime juice*
- *10ml fresh white grapefruit juice*
- *10ml Kirsch dry cherry liqueur*
- ***Garnish:*** *orange peel twist*

Shake all ingredients with ice. Strain into a wine goblet over freshly crushed ice. Express orange oils and add an orange peel twist.

AN ECUMENICAL MATTER

From Aqua Vitae's inception for its medicinal attributes in 1324, to the first notes in 1350 of the Bishops' cabinets being locked due to unscheduled consumption in various dioceses, there has been the Ecumenical Matter of want versus need, leading to the eventual replication for personal consumption and enjoyment outside of the medicinal properties.

Sip... Savour... Repent...

- *30ml port blend (50:50 tawny:ruby)*
- *30ml Aqua Vitae*
- *10ml yellow chartreuse*
- *4 dashes of marmalade citrus bitters*
- ***Garnish:*** *orange peel twist*

Place all ingredients in a mixing glass with ice. Stir and serve over block ice. Express orange oils over top and garnish with an orange peel twist.

PRESCRIPTION TODDY

Through this drink, we can acknowledge the receipt of medicinal reasons as to why a hot whiskey is prescribed as a home remedy in times of a cold snap. Hot water to kill the impurities, honey for energy reserves, the warming spices of Aqua Vitae to open the vocal chords to breathe and its strength to break a fever. Its calming scented lemon oils to relax the imbiber and the experience to bring hence a flutter back to one's heart.

- *40ml Aqua Vitae*
- *15ml honey syrup*
- *4 dashes of hedgerow aromatic bitters*
- *150ml hot water*
- ***Garnish:*** *lemon peel twist*

Place all ingredients in a glass. Express oils from a lemon peel over top, twist and drop inside.

MÍL GIN

Míl is an Irish pot still gin, distilled with fragrant Mediterranean botanicals. Distilled with almond, basil, bergamot orange, gooseberry, juniper, olives, orris, rosemary and thyme, this small batch gin is bursting with southern sunshine.

Míl was created by a team of 'ginthusiasts' at the Pearse Lyons Distillery, in the refurbished St James' Church, who were moved by the historic site links with the Camino de Santiago in north-west Spain where tradition has it St James is buried.

This gin is an Iberian-Irish fusion, personified through the story of Míl, the mythical Spanish warrior whose descendants populated Ireland bringing with them the warm flavours of the sun.

MEDITERRANEAN SNAPPER

A Mediterranean version of a Bloody Mary, it uses gin and sherry instead of vodka with a subtle addition of balsamic vinegar. It's a real tomato explosion and a perfect hangover cure too!

- *40ml Míl Gin*
- *15ml Pedro Ximénez sherry*
- *3 dashes balsamic vinegar*
- *120ml tomato juice*
- *15ml lime juice*
- *Pinch of celery salt & black pepper*
- ***Garnish:*** *cherry tomatoes & basil leaf*

Put all ingredients into a cocktail shaker filled with ice. Shake until very cold. Pour into a tall glass with ice. Garnish with cherry tomatoes and a basil leaf.

ROE & CO WHISKEY

Roe & Co Distilling Company is a modern Irish whiskey distillery, with its heart in methodical science and creative collaborations.

Roe & Co is named in honour of George Roe, the once world-famous whiskey maker who helped build the golden era of Irish whiskey in the 19th century. The story is inspired by the past success of the Irish whiskey category but is also informed by its mistakes.

'As we revive this category and the legacy of brewing and distilling in the Liberties of Dublin, we are working tirelessly to usher in the new Golden Era.'

Roe & Co was born out of a partnership between Diageo Master Blender Caroline Martin and five Ireland-based bartenders, with the task of creating a unique blended Irish whiskey that would hold its own neat, in mixed drinks and cocktails. In the true spirit of collaboration and endurance, this vastly experienced team trialled over 106 prototype blends to create this truly extraordinary expression of Irish whiskey.

Roe & Co is an Irish whiskey made by bartenders for bartenders and as such, they will always be a key partner in sharing the Roe & Co story.

Flavour profile: Roe & Co is an elegant Irish whiskey, packed with delicious layers of flavour including vanilla, caramel and spiced orchard fruits. A masterful blend of rich malt and smooth grain whiskeys aged in a high proportion of first-fill bourbon barrels gives this Irish whiskey depth of flavour.

ROE HIGHBALL

It's a classic and simple way to enjoy your favourite whiskey. One of the world's simplest yet most sophisticated drinks.

- *50ml Roe & Co Whiskey*
- *20ml lemon juice*
- *10ml sugar syrup*
- *Soda water*
- *Sprig of rosemary*
- ***Garnish:*** *sprig of rosemary*

Shake the whiskey with a sprig of rosemary, lemon juice and sugar syrup. Fine strain into a highball glass, top with soda and garnish with a sprig of rosemary.

THE GM

The well-balanced combination of sweet, sour and bitter makes the GM a fresh and seriously delicious summer cocktail.

- *30ml Roe & Co Whiskey*
- *20ml Belsazar Rose*
- *15ml sugar syrup*
- *60ml fresh grapefruit juice*
- *10ml fresh lime juice*
- ***Garnish:** sprig of rosemary*

Shake and strain into a salt rimmed glass over ice. Garnish with a sprig of rosemary. Pour a small drop of Talisker over the drink for fragrance.

CARETAKER

This rhubarb and ginger creation is a seasonal explosion of flavour and a modern take on a classic favourite.

- *40ml Roe & Co Whiskey*
- *60ml salted Verdejo*
- *25ml rhubarb & ginger syrup*
- *2 dashes rhubarb bitters*
- *Soda water*
- ***Garnish:*** *rhubarb ribbon*

Build all ingredients in a highball glass over ice. Gently stir. Garnish with a rhubarb ribbon.

BLACKWATER GIN

Founded by friends Peter Mulryan and Kieran Curtin in 2014, Blackwater Distillery is a micro-distillery based in west Waterford on the banks of the Blackwater River.

'We like to keep it real, which is why early in the morning we switch on the lights, open the post and fire up the still. In our 1950s-converted hardware store in Ballyduff, we make award-winning gin and small batch Irish whisky.'

The distillery is located in one of Ireland's best kept secrets ' – The Blackwater Region – and it takes its name from the nearby Blackwater River. In Irish, its name is 'An Abhainn Mhór' or 'The Big River' and big it certainly is. Sometimes referred to as the Munster Blackwater, it rises on the Cork-Kerry border and flows due east into Waterford, flowing past the distillery in Ballyduff. It makes an abrupt right turn at Cappoquin, is joined by its tributary river, the Bride, and flows into the sea at Youghal. 'It is the historic connection between Waterford and more exotic climes that inspires our gins.'

Today the Blackwater is famous as a salmon river but for hundreds of years its deep dark waters made it a perfect artery of commerce. From Sir Walter Raleigh with his potato and tobacco, to the current Duke of Devonshire in Lismore Castle, this part of Ireland has long traded with the farthest corners of the globe.

In Victorian times, Whites of Waterford was the largest spice importer in the country, and they grew wealthy shipping everything from sugar to cinnamon into the region. Also, the first steamboat in Ireland was on the backwater, as were the last sailing schooners to travel waters between Ireland and Britain.

BEE RIGHT WITH YOU

This award-winning cocktail celebrates all things local. The creator sees cocktails not just bringing together ingredients but businesses as well, both big and small. He always uses Irish spirits and looks for locally-grown produce. The cocktail won Best Irish Cocktail 2018.

- *50ml Blackwater No5 Gin*
- *2 dashes bitters*
- *Juice of 1 lime & 1 lemon*
- *2tsp good local honey*
- *1 egg white*
- ***Garnish**: edible flowers*

Combine all ingredients in a shaker. Shake for a long time until honey runs free. Strain into a glass. Garnish with edible flowers.

Recipe by: John Coleman, Grand Hotel, Fermoy

WATERFORD WHISKY

Influenced by the world's greatest winemakers, Waterford Distillery obsessively brings the same intellectual drive, methodology and rigour to single malt whisky.

Their Single Farm Origin showcases barley flavours derived from individual Irish farms, terroir by terroir, each a single malt in its own right. They are expressions of precision and rarity. Yet, gathered together into a cuvée, layer by layer, these component spirits create a definitive and complex single malt. 'Our ultimate goal: the world's most unique, complex and profound whisky.'

In Ireland's sunny south east, warmed by the Gulf Stream, temperate, moist air crosses fertile soils to produce a verdant landscape – and the world's finest barley. Since barley is the source of malt whisky's complex flavours, it makes sense to focus on where and how the barley is cultivated. Those flavours are shaped by place, by the soils that nourish its roots, and by the microclimate in which it ripens – by terroir.

There's been a brewery on the banks of the River Suir since 1792. Today's Waterford Distillery, the technological marvel they call the Facilitator, enables them to create elite whisky. They keep each farm's crop demonstrably separate and treated equally as they transform it from grain to spirit.

State-of-the-art equipment marries with ancient knowledge, local Irish barley with extended 120-hour fermentations, unhurried distillation with a spectrum of exceptional oak. In this way they can reveal the ultimate expression of terroir, farm by farm, harvest by harvest. Unique distillates, new starting points and beguiling expressions of place.

After maturing for several years in the best of French and American oak – a wood policy so costly and unparalleled that it accounts for one third of their production budget – they believe these component single malts - a solo voice, a solo terroir, each one exhibiting its own nuances - will come together as a glorious chorus of harmonic flavours. The total of the sum of its parts.

'This is how, we humbly believe, the most profound single malt whisky ever can be created. And that remains our ambition. Our destination. Our whole raison d'être.'

MISSION FIG

Rich, sweet and warm notes of both whiskey and fig complement each other beautifully in this cosy take on a classic favourite.

- *60ml Waterford Whisky*
- *10ml fig syrup*
- *3 dashes black walnut bitters*
- **Garnish:** *orange peel, fig wedge & sprig of thyme*

In a whiskey glass, combine the fig syrup and bitters. Add a large ice cube and stir. Squeeze the orange peel to extract oils and drop it in the glass. Add the whiskey and stir again. Garnish with a fig wedge, orange peel and a sprig of thyme.

ACKNOWLEDGEMENTS

Most importantly, I want to thank the wonderful Irish spirit makers for inspiring me to publish *Craft Cocktails* and for being a part of it. Thank you for your enthusiasm!

To Dave and Andy of two award-winning cocktail bars - Bar 1661 in Dublin and Cask in Cork - thank you for collaborating with me and contributing to this book. You guys are legends!

A very special thanks to the super talented Aoibhne Hogan of Greet Street for stunning illustrations and design. I couldn't possibly love it more!

Brenda, thank you so much for editing and proofreading the book on such a tight timeline. I owe you dinner and a few cocktails!

Last but not least, I want to thank my husband, Fergus, for always supporting my dreams and aspirations. Massive thanks to you and my dear friends and family for believing in this book!

INDEX

INDEX

INDEX

INDEX